Sewer Inspector

BY ARNOLD RINGSTAD

Published in the United States of America by The Child's World®
1980 Lookout Drive • Mankato, MN 56003-1705
800-599-READ • www.childsworld.com

Acknowledgments
The Child's World®: Mary Berendes, Publishing Director
Red Line Editorial: Editorial direction
The Design Lab: Design
Amnet: Production

Photographs ©: LightTheBox/Thinkstock, cover; lifehouseimage/
Thinkstock, 5; Pavel L Photo and Video/Shutterstock Images,
6; Steve Remich/AP Images, 9; Fanch Galivel/Thinkstock, 10;
Luke MacGregor/Corbis, 12; Library of Congress, 15; Jovana
Milanko/Thinkstock, 16; Liz Mangelsdorf/Corbis, 19; Alexandru
Magurean/Thinkstock, 20

ISBN 9781631436918
LCCN 2014945303

Printed in the United States of America
Mankato, MN
November, 2014
PA02238

ABOUT THE AUTHOR

Arnold Ringstad lives in Minnesota, where he writes and edits books for kids. He enjoys reading about the history of sewers, roads, and other important parts of cities.

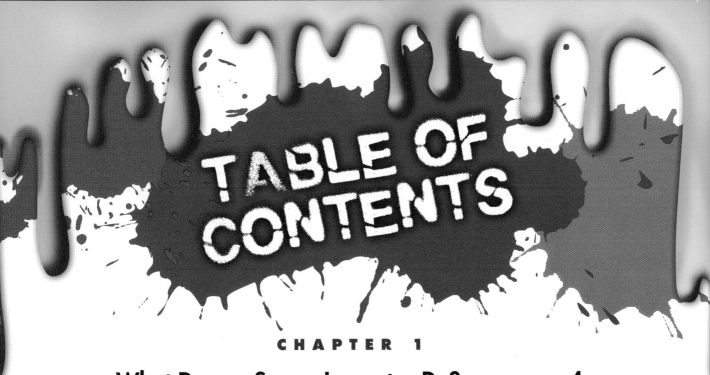

TABLE OF CONTENTS

CHAPTER 1

What Does a Sewer Inspector Do?. 4

CHAPTER 2

A Day on the Job 8

CHAPTER 3

Why Cleaning Sewers Is Important 14

CHAPTER 4

Overcoming Problems. 18

Glossary 22

To Learn More 23

Index 24

What Does a Sewer Inspector Do?

Sewer inspectors keep cities clean. Water that leaves homes is dirty. Waste flows down from bathrooms. Dirt gets in from showers. Food scraps come in from sinks. Pipes carry dirty water away. But where does it go next?

Sewers are systems of pipes. They collect a city's dirty water. They also collect rainwater. The water is carried to **treatment plants**. It is cleaned. Then it can be used for other things.

DISGUSTING!
Sewers often smell like rotten eggs. A poisonous gas causes the smell. It comes from the waste in the sewer.

Sewers often have walkways for workers to use so they don't have to walk through the waste.

Inspectors make sure pipes are working. Pipes could break. Water could leak. Dirty water could mix with drinking water. This would make the water unsafe to drink. Dirty water could also spill onto streets. This could make people sick. Inspectors stop this from happening.

Being a sewer inspector is difficult. Sewers usually smell awful. An inspector may have to work at odd hours.

Rushing waters are one of the greatest dangers sewer inspectors face.

Sometimes they have to do emergency inspections. Storms or broken pipes cause problems. Inspectors work in all types of weather. Working underground protects against some weather. But rain means inspectors must work in rushing water.

Workers must know how to use technology. Cameras and computers look through sewers. Workers control them from the surface. Still, inspectors often must get dirty.

Inspectors need special skills. They should be good at math. They need to be able to read **blueprints**. This helps them understand the sewer system. They may need to take a test to become an inspector.

DISGUSTING!
In 2005, a 10-foot (3-m) snake crawled through sewers in England! It even entered homes through the toilet. It was finally caught on a bathroom floor.

CHAPTER 2

A Day on the Job

Workers first figure out which sewers need inspection. They hear about problems people are having. Sometimes people's sinks do not drain. Sewer smells can enter homes. These may be signs of sewer trouble. Inspectors check nearby sewers.

Cleaning a sewer makes inspection easier. Workers use flusher trucks that have huge tanks of water. Pumps push the water at high speed through hoses. Workers lower the hoses into the sewer. They spray the sides of the sewer. They drag the hose out slowly so that the water sprays the whole sewer. Then they are ready to enter. Workers often enter through a **manhole**. They climb a ladder down into the sewer.

Bugs, rats, and other animals live in the sewer. It may seem gross to work next to these creatures. But workers like to see animals. If animals are alive down there, it means it is

This robotic sewer inspector has lights and a camera its operators use to find and record any damage in the pipes.

safe. Finding dead animals would be a warning sign. It could mean there is poison gas.

Workers sometimes send cameras into the sewers. Using cameras to find problems means that workers don't have to go into the sewers. But cameras are expensive and can be difficult to set up.

Seeing a sewer in person is often better than using a camera. It gives the clearest view. Workers can get close to

Inspectors need to enter dark and dirty places to assess the whole sewer.

the sewer walls so they can spot small problems. They can measure things or take close-up photos. They later study the photos to find problems.

Inspectors look for several kinds of problems. Fractures are breaks that go all the way through pipes. Cracks are smaller breaks that do not go all the way through. Another problem is **deformation**. This is when the pipe flattens out. Less water can flow through. One serious problem is

collapse. Collapses may stop the flow of water. Collapses need repairs right away.

One big problem in sewers is slow water flow. **Grease** can block the water. Many people put grease down drains. The grease hardens as it cools. It sticks to sewer walls. The grease builds over time. It starts to block the water. Restaurants produce a lot of grease. They must use grease traps in sinks. These stop grease from going down the drain. Inspectors watch out for grease in sewers. They may use water or chemicals to wash it away.

Inspectors also look for other problems. Surface damage happens when the insides of pipes get damaged. This can be caused by chemicals. The problem may not be serious right away.

TECHNOLOGY

A new type of **sensor** makes inspection easier. It hangs from manhole covers. It senses if the water gets too high. This could mean a problem with the sewer. The sensor alerts inspectors.

Inspectors wear protective clothing to keep themselves safe and make their jobs easier.

Inspectors check if the damage increases over time. Inspectors also watch for tree roots. Roots can break through pipes.

Inspectors take samples of concrete pipes. They study the samples in a laboratory. This lets them test the pipe's strength. Many old concrete pipes have problems. Concrete was once poured differently. The way it was poured can leave holes. Inspectors find out if the concrete needs repair.

Inspecting sewers in person is useful. However, other kinds of inspection may be needed, too. It can be hard for workers to see below the water. Sometimes workers can't reach problem spots. They use a camera in these situations. Cameras are placed on floating platforms. They move through the sewer. Workers control the camera from the surface. Other devices can even detect problems underwater. They use **sonar**. A sonar device makes a sound underwater. Then it listens for the echo. It measures how long it takes for the echo to return. This creates a picture of what it looks like underwater. Workers examine it for problems.

Why Cleaning Sewers Is Important

Removing wastewater is an ancient idea. Some people once simply threw dirty water out of windows. This led to health problems. People later realized it is important to remove waste. Many large cities had sewers by the late 1800s. Pipes carried water to and from homes.

Early sewers were sometimes open to the air. Wastewater could spill out onto the streets. It mixed with drinking water. This made people sick. Designers made closed pipes to stop leaks.

But waste was still entering rivers. Soon, people realized cities downstream were getting sick. Their drinking water was dirty. In the 1900s, people figured out solutions. First, they piped wastewater to treatment plants instead of rivers.

Open sewers, like this one in San Juan, Puerto Rico, in 1938, spilled waste into drinking water and caused disease.

And second, they cleaned their drinking water before giving it to people. Fewer people got sick.

But modern sewers have problems, too. Broken sewers can't carry waste safely. Inspectors make sure sewers

DISGUSTING!

London, England, had open sewers in 1858. In that year, waste collected in the Thames River. As it sat in the hot sun, it smelled awful. The summer of 1858 was known as the "Great Stink."

Inspectors access sewers through manholes.

are working correctly. Even new sewers are inspected. Some problems happen when old parts break down. But many problems come from new pieces. Sometimes they are built wrong. They may be installed wrong. Workers want to find these problems right away.

It's important to catch problems early. Large sewer pipes are expensive to fix. Repairs may disrupt streets. Big pipes are often below roads. Workers close roads to work on the sewers. They may even dig up the street. This can close off part of the city for months. This is one reason why inspection is important. Inspectors catch small problems before they become big. Fixing a small problem may be cheap. Fixing a large problem is expensive.

Some underground pipes can be huge. Some are even big enough to drive a car through! They are also long. Large cities have many miles of pipe. New York City has about 2,200 miles (3,540 km) of sewers for waste water. That's longer than the Appalachian Trail from Maine to Georgia! Another 1,820 miles (2,930 km) are just for storm water.

CHAPTER 4

Overcoming Problems

Sewers are dangerous places. Harmful gases can fill sewers. **Bacteria** can make workers sick. The smell makes it uncomfortable. Slippery sewers can cause painful falls.

Workers take steps to stay safe. First, they train for their work. They prepare safety plans. They know what to do if a disaster happens. The sewer could collapse while workers are inside. A worker could get hurt underground. Inspectors plan for these disasters.

Workers carry gear to keep them safe. Special clothing protects them from dirty water. Masks let them breathe in the sewer. Workers carry first aid kits in case of emergencies. They use powerful flashlights to see. Workers also use devices that check the air for dangerous gases. This tells them if it's safe to enter the sewer.

Sediment can build up on the floor of sewers, making the already small tunnels even shorter.

It is dangerous to enter a sewer during wet weather.

Inspectors use radios to talk to each other. Workers on the surface must be able to talk to workers in the sewers. This is especially important in emergencies.

Rain makes inspection more difficult. It can also be dangerous. Workers can slip and fall if water flows through the sewer. They must watch the weather. They usually enter the sewers only when it is dry outside. Sometimes workers must enter the sewer when it is rainy. They may need to do an emergency inspection. If this happens, they use special gear to keep safe.

Sometimes sewers fill with water. When this happens, inspectors need diving suits. They swim through the pipes. This is very dangerous. Workers must bring air to breathe. They need extra training to stay safe.

Sewer inspectors do a lot of gross work. But they make the world less gross for everyone else. They make sure waste is disposed of safely.

TECHNOLOGY

It can be tough to move through sewers. It is especially hard when workers carry equipment. One team in Canada found a solution. They built a small three-wheeled car. It carries workers and equipment. It moves through sewers just 5 feet (1.5 m) wide.

GLOSSARY

bacteria (bak-TEER-ee-uh) Bacteria are tiny living things that can cause diseases. Many bacteria live in sewers.

blueprints (BLOO-prints) Blueprints are drawn plans for structures or objects. Inspectors look at sewer blueprints to see how the pipes fit together.

grease (GREES) Grease is oil or fat used for cooking. Grease often clogs sewer pipes.

sensor (SEN-sur) A sensor is a device that detects something. A special sensor can tell workers if water levels in sewers are rising.

sonar (SOH-nahr) Sonar is a system that bounces sound off surfaces to learn what is going on underwater. Sewer inspectors can use sonar to assess the condition of the sewer below the water level.

treatment plants (TREET-mint plants) Treatment plants are places where dirty water is cleaned. Sewers carry waste from homes and businesses to treatment plants.

TO LEARN MORE

BOOKS

Cole, Joanna. *The Magic School Bus at the Waterworks.*
New York: Scholastic, 2004.

Horn, Geoffrey. *Sewer Inspector.* New York:
Marshall Cavendish Benchmark, 2011.

WEB SITES

Visit our Web site for links about sewer inspectors:
childsworld.com/links

*Note to Parents, Teachers, and Librarians: We routinely verify our Web links to make
sure they are safe and active sites. So encourage your readers to check them out!*

INDEX

cameras, 7, 9, 13
cities, 4, 14, 17

drinking water, 5, 14, 15

gear, 18, 21

health problems, 5, 14, 15, 18

manholes, 8, 11

pipes, 4, 5, 7, 10, 11, 13, 14, 17, 21

smell, 4, 5, 8, 15, 18

treatment plants, 4, 14

waste, 4, 14, 15, 17, 21
weather, 7, 20, 21